KATIE DOWNING

8 Easy (& Cheap) Ways to Improve Your Website

A Quick Guide: UX, SEO & Content DIY Tips to Optimize Your Site for Organic Search and a Better User Experience

First edition

This book was professionally typeset on Reedsy.
Find out more at reedsy.com

Contents

1   Introduction   1

2   Spy on Your Competitors   5

3   Does Your Website Work?   8

4   Your Main Menu Navigation   12

5   Give Your Visitors a Call to Action (CTA)   14

6   Website Writing   17

7   Formatting & Optimizing is Crucial   26

8   Optimize Your Blog   33

9   Harness the Impact of SEO   39

10   Questions to Ask Your SEO Pro or Agency   52

11   Local SEO & Google Business Profile   57

12   Last Thoughts   60

13   Resources   62

1

Introduction

Your website is an extension of your brand, your company... you. It's a vessel to bring in customers (or your audience), and it never stops working for you.

Until it does.

What if I told you there were 8 effective things you could do to improve your website, provide a better experience for your users, have a stronger organic search presence, and that you can do it yourself with free tools?

As a content and copywriter, editor, SEO professional and digital marketer since 2007, I geek out over optimizing websites. It hurts my heart when I see a horrible UX experience, lack of basic on-page SEO tactics, or weak content.

A moderately seasoned SEO professional or content writer would know these tips, so none of this is a big secret. They would do more advanced techniques with more expensive tools.

Oh, and they would charge you a lot to do it.

I'm not trying to take business away from my fellow SEO tribe. They are very talented people. I still work every day on websites, in SEO and digital content.

Don't misunderstand me. Hiring the right pro SEO person to optimize your website and help you build organic search traffic is absolutely worth it. I am by no means implying that you shouldn't do so.

The reason I wrote this book is because I understand how confusing these topics can be for someone who doesn't live in the world of search, content, or UX design.

SEO is one of the highest searched topics, and there are smarter people than me writing books and posting on LinkedIn about SEO and website optimization. But it can be overwhelming to sift through the advice... the jargon... the lessons.

Not to mention the back-and-forth discussions and opinions of how these topics should be executed.

I want to share my perspective on the matter and show you how UX, SEO, and content are all interconnected. I've compiled the things that anyone with any experience can do — things I've done to help my clients' websites perform better.

I've seen the impact of organic search (and that Google has too much power). I understand managing a website can be daunting. And the quickly changing internet environment is hard to keep up with.

Whether you're a small business owner who doesn't know what to do with your website, or a blogger, or a non-profit organization, or you just want to reach your fan base of Beanie Baby collectors, (not judging) the tips in this book can help improve your site so it works *for* you and helps connect you to your audience.

This is meant to be a quick guide to get you started.

I recommend you read it from cover to cover first because so many of these steps are intertwined.

There are a lot of free resources available and referenced throughout the chapters and put on the Resources page at the end.

The items in this book can be done in waves. The best thing about digital is you can always adjust as you go, when you need to change something, or if you see a mistake or areas of improvement.

Important: Do not make your adjustments directly on your site. Do it on paper first — a Word Doc or Google Doc. That way you don't risk screwing up your site while you're working on it. And you can take a more holistic approach to your changes. Plus, it's easier to check spelling and grammar when Word or Google Doc points it out to you.

It's always a good idea to have a backup of your site before you

start making adjustments. Your CMS may do this already, but the more you know, right?

Also of note: If you have an agency or person implementing these optimizations, I recommend you review your contract so you know what they will charge you to make these changes. (I am not legally bound to pay your fees for you. Ha.)

I would also recommend you give them your changes chunks at a time or figure out everything you want changed/adjusted at once and send it to them versus "change this sentence" and then go back to them later and say, "change this button". It may be cheaper to go to them one time instead of multiple times.

Even if you do have someone managing your website, writing, or doing SEO, you can still use this book to educate yourself on what to look for on your site and check their work.

There is a chapter on questions you can ask the agency or person you're using. Hopefully this can give you confidence to have those conversations if needed. Or use the information just for your own knowledge.

You don't need to be an expert in any of these areas. Just keep it simple. And always, always, always look at it from your user's point of view. (And check your work.)

With that, let's get to it!

2

Spy on Your Competitors

It's not spying if it's in the name of research. Checking out your competitors' websites is very telling. If they have an unprofessional website, making the adjustments from this book should help you compete or surpass them in organic search and provide a better experience for your visitors (and maybe you will get their visitors as well!).

Only pick 2-3 competitors. It's easy to fall down the rabbit hole of competitor research and before you know it, you've wasted hours.

Don't waste hours.

Give yourself an hour. Maybe 2. But don't go longer than that. It gets daunting.

If you don't have local competitors or you're not sure what's out there, do a quick Google search for your product or service and see what comes up. You can include your city in the search:

"office chairs Tucson".

Even if you don't search in your area, you can still find a lot of good takeaways.

You can also use the free version of BrightLocal. This is a tool you can try for 14 days without entering a credit card. You add a keyword or phrase into the search bar — like your product or service — input your city and state, and it will show you an organic Google search in your local area. It's a helpful way to find local competitors.

Here are some things to look for:

1. Can you tell what service they provide?
2. What problem do they solve for customers or clients or patients or whatever the audience is?
3. Is their content engaging? Is it user-focused or is it all about themselves?
4. Can you navigate the website easily? Is it clear what they want you to do?
5. What navigation items do they use in their main menu?
6. What does it look like on your phone? What about your desktop?
7. Do they use good photos?
8. What do you like about the website?
9. What don't you like?

Don't take too much time looking through their websites, but jot down notes for each one and then compile the results. Make a list of the things you like and may want to try for your own website.

Maybe they had a page that you don't have, and you think it would be useful. (Keep in mind that too many navigation items in your menu can be cumbersome. Just keep it simple and include what helps the user.)

The list of bad things you found is just as important. These are items you need to steer clear of on your own site or fix if you have the same issue.

We will do another competitor analysis later when we talk about keywords, so make sure you document what websites you looked at.

Now that you know what others are doing, you are armed with knowledge of what you could implement and what you should ditch on your own site.

3

Does Your Website Work?

Have you tried to purchase something online only to get an error message that more than likely didn't provide the necessary information to tell you what exactly went wrong?

Or you were sent an email that had a link to get something or do something, only to find the link took you to a page that didn't exist?

Super annoying, right? Talk about road rage — digital style.

I don't know who your audience is, but your website is a connection point. If they have a good experience, they will return, share it with their family and friends — hopefully on social media — and associate sunshine and rainbows with your service. (Okay, so we don't live in a Disney movie, but you get my point.)

One bad moment on your site could turn them away forever. No sharing of how awesome you or your business is, no returning.

They will just go somewhere else.

Yes, I'm being a bit dramatic, but I can't stress enough how crucial your website is.

This is why functionality is the first step in improving your website. Does your site work?

Depending on how big your website is, you want to check every page and link to see if it takes you to the place it's supposed to. If you have social buttons or links in the footer, click on each one and make sure it goes to the right social platform. (Don't forget to swap out the Twitter icon for the X icon.)

Every page in your navigation main menu must go to the correct page. Any "Shop Now" or "Learn More" or "Schedule an Appointment" button must work properly.

If you sell products, check each product link, and make sure it is the correct product, that it goes in the cart if you click it, etc.

Enlist family or friends to help you with your quality check. Write down a few tasks for them to do and have them document their experience.

For example: "Visit the website from the homepage, find this product, and purchase it."

You may need to give them the funds to do it or don't have them actually put in the credit card information. (This is a step you want to run smoothly, so making sure it's not a cumbersome process or that there's an error in set up is important.) Adjust this to fit your services.

Or have them "Visit the site from the homepage and schedule an appointment." See if they run into any roadblocks.

If you're thinking, "I sell over 100 products. I'm not going to click on each one manually..." I get it. It's okay. Call in some favors. Split them up and have your family and friends each take 10-20, or you can run your site through a software program like Screaming Frog or Ahrefs which pulls each of your page links and can show you things that are wrong.

However, if you go this route, you may not be able to use the free version of these tools. Or they may only allow restricted access or require and they aren't cheap.

If you have a small site, you don't need these programs. They can be expensive and challenging to navigate.

But this isn't meant to be a cumbersome project. Its purpose is to make sure your website is working the way it's supposed to when visitors come.

You can use Excel or Google Sheets to list your pages and add the date when you check the links. This will be useful if you do another check in 6 months or a year. Or if someone lets you know of a broken link, you can look back at the date you last checked it and determine how long it may have been broken.

This is a quality check process that every business, educational institution, non-profit — you name it — does before their website goes live (or shortly thereafter). It's a standard industry process and so, so important.

Once you know your website functions the way it's meant to, then you can move on with confidence to the next step.

4

Your Main Menu Navigation

Chances are high that the first thing a person does on a website is look at the navigation menu at the top or in the hamburger menu (the three horizontal lines you often see as the menu on your phone). This is the map of your site. It helps your visitor navigate to where they need to be.

Don't clutter it up. Keep it simple.

What did you notice about your competitors' websites?

How many pages did they include in their navigation?

Did any seem like they didn't need to be there?

Have you ever visited a website that had so many items in a dropdown menu that it was too hard to find what you needed or didn't format correctly on your phone?

Again, keep it simple. Only put in the navigation what makes sense and what's needed.

Keep your labels short. No need to put "Our Products". Just use "Products". Don't use "Subscribe to our Newsletter". Just put "Subscribe". Save the "Subscribe to our Newsletter" for a CTA or a header on the newsletter subscription page.

Here are the basic pages you could have:

- Home (obviously)
- About Us
- Contact/Location
- Services/Products/What you offer
- Subscribe/Order
- Blog/Resources

Navigation items 100% rely on the industry, product, or service you provide. If you currently have a lot of items in your menu, see what you can remove and just put it as a link on the main page.

Be careful not to remove a menu item and then forget to add a link somewhere on the page.

The goal is to make your navigation simple with the most important items included. It should be a guide to navigate your site, not a catch-all for every page you have.

5

Give Your Visitors a Call to Action (CTA)

What is a CTA? It's your call to action. It's what you want your website visitor to do at that moment on that page.

The CTA is dependent on your industry or service you provide. A CTA can include a "Buy Now" or "Get Yours Today" button. Or it could be a "Schedule Your Appointment". Perhaps it's an email sign up or a "Download Your Copy Here". It can be a button or linked text.

The point of the CTA is that your customer, patient, volunteer, client, or visitor doesn't leave your website without taking an action — preferably the one you strategically put in their path.

If they do take this action, it's called a conversion and leads them down your marketing funnel as a paying customer, a donor, a lead, an appointment, and so on.

Your visitor needs to be guided. Show them what to do. But don't make the CTA too long or too generic.

When you have a page full of "Read More" or "Learn More", it gets redundant, distracting, and it doesn't tell your users or search engines what's on the other side of that link.

Do this: Go through your homepage and decide what it is you want your visitors to do. It can be one or two things, maybe three depending on what you have on your homepage.

For instance, you could have a section that showcases your latest three blogs. It would make sense to have a CTA of "See More Topics Here" that links to your blog page. Or if you have a product or service you're highlighting, "Browse Our Products" and link to the product page.

If you have a non-profit, maybe it makes sense to include a CTA that says, "Become a Volunteer", "Make a Difference Now" or "Make Your Donation Today".

Use your supporting text around the CTA to help explain it. If you want people to "Help Us Move Forward" or "Help Us Help Others", explain in a concise manner how they can do that.

Keep a lookout for any CTAs that can be punched up with better action words that are user focused vs organization or company focused. (See Web Writing chapter.)

Take notice if you have too many CTAs flying around a page. You don't want to have competing options for the user to choose from. Obviously, there are exceptions.

For example, an ecommerce site must have CTAs for each

product on the page. A small business that sells a service vs a product may have different CTA needs. A homepage may need multiple CTAs to help the user find areas of possible interest.

Bottom line, figure out what you want them to do on each page and write the action CTA to get them to convert.

Pay attention to the contrast of the button and the font color of the text in the CTA. See the formatting chapter on colored links later on.

P.S. Do not use "Click here". Ever. The end.

6

Website Writing

What is your content like? Perhaps it's short and sparse. Maybe you have big block paragraphs that ramble on. Is it valuable to your user?

When you were looking at competitor websites, what did you notice?

Was the copy engaging?

Did you feel like they were talking to you or at you?

Or do you feel like they were talking about themselves and how great they were?

User-Focused Content

This is one thing that a lot of organizations get wrong. They want to brag about how amazing they are. And they are. They do a lot of great things. Impressive things.

But that's not why the visitor is there. The user wants to know how a company, organization, or non-profit can help them solve their problem. That's what you must have in mind as you're looking at your content — an honest look at your content.

How do you write with the user in mind?

Ditch "we" and "our" and replace it with "you" and "your". You need to show them how your products or services benefit them.

Example of a "we" statement: We were voted the best pants in Ohio!

Try: You voted our pants the best in Ohio. Thank you! It is because of you that we're able to offer...

The most important thing to keep in mind is to write about the benefit of the product or service versus the features. You can include features, but the focus should be the benefit to the user.

Active vs Passive Voice

Learn the difference between active and passive voice. It will help you get rid of the fluff and be more direct in your writing. Even the most seasoned writers catch themselves on this one.

In fact, I guarantee I use passive voice in this book.

Here's an overly simplified way to tell if you use passive vs active: "ing".

If you start a sentence with "ing" in the word, chances are it uses passive voice. In short, find the most direct way to say something without sacrificing flow, voice, or conversational tone.

Read more about this topic on the Grammarly blog. (See the resources page at the end of this book.)

Writing for the Web & Mobile

Usually, you can delete any first paragraph you ever write on a page because your stronger paragraph is typically your second one. That's because as you start to write a page, it's common to use fluff in the first paragraph.

Keep it short.

Keep it brief.

Keep it engaging.

Keep it conversational.

Give them a hook.

This is the first thing they're going to see on your page. A strong headline is a way to relate to them. Give it a little personality. Don't use big words just because you want to sound intelligent. Write like you speak — like your audience speaks. (But maybe less "dude" and "bro".)

Cut down your sentences.

For digital writing, you should not have three or four long sentences. They should be varied. Sometimes you need a longer complex sentence. Sometimes you need shorter ones.

Break up your text. Do not have one big block of text. Not only is this a horrible experience, but it is too hard to read on mobile, and your users just won't read it.

You must write for the readers, the skimmers, and the search engines. You'll see posts on LinkedIn of SEO pros saying you don't write for Google. That's true and it's not.

You write for your audience, while keeping in mind that Google wants quality content that's easy to digest.

How do you write for all three of these?

Do the things I mentioned above — varied sentences. Use bullets and numbered lists when it makes sense to do so. (I'll talk more about this in the formatting chapter.)

People love bullets because they're in a hurry, and their attention spans are short. They want to get the information they need quickly. Google and search engines also love bullets for the same reason.

It doesn't have to be perfect, and you don't have to do every page at once. Find a website with content you like. Maybe it's how they formatted it. Maybe it's the tone and the voice. Try to mirror that. (Mirror, don't steal.)

The great thing about digital is it's not set in stone. You can try something. If you don't like it, you can try it again. Adjust it as you go. That's the beauty of a website.

The biggest thing is to be clear about what you want them to do on that page. Don't clutter it up with a bunch of extra information that your customer, patient, visitor, or volunteer doesn't need to know.

This isn't a high school report or a research paper for college. You can have some fun with this. Again, depending on your industry, or your product or service, you may need to be a little bit more informal in some instances. Otherwise, just write as you speak.

ChatGPT & AI

Yes, you can use ChatGPT and AI programs to help you write your website. But I will say this — move forward with caution. This isn't something you can just use with your eyes closed.

Things to consider:

- Your prompts need to be clear about what you want.
- You MUST check your work — it's your responsibility to ensure the content is not plagiarized and that it's accurate.
- You can use plagiarism software like Grammarly.com.
- You can't just take what the AI program writes and use it verbatim. AI can write sentences that sound unnatural and

non-conversational.
- You will also need to proofread it.
- If you use ChatGPT to write some content, make sure the tone and voice matches the rest of your site.

Product & Service Descriptions

Descriptions for products and services is a topic that could fit in multiple places in this book. I put it here in the Web Writing section because I want to make sure you include this in your plan if your site needs it.

When you get to the keyword section of the SEO chapter, you will apply those tips to the descriptions.

Label your products so they are easy to remember — don't do what a hardware store does and use a bunch of numbers and product IDs.

Use keywords where appropriate in your description of the product. Keep it concise but think about what the customer may want to know in order to purchase this item.

Internal Jargon vs Real Speak

I'll be brief. Don't use internal jargon. Your audience doesn't care and won't know what you're talking about.

Absolutely use industry terms your users would understand. It adds validity to what you do and builds trust.

Highlighter Test

The highlighter test is a great way to see how often you use a certain word or start a sentence with the same word. Pick one highlighter color (either on your digital document or a real highlighter if you print the pages out). Go through your pages and highlight when you use a particular word.

For example, let's say you start three sentences in one paragraph with "This". This is... This has... This product... for a reader, that can be distracting (unless it's done stylistically to prove a point. I used "Keep" four times in a sentence earlier in this chapter. It was intentional.) Highlight "This" every time you use it.

Then pick a different highlighter color and do the same thing for another word. "Because" and "that" are popular ones. You would also do this same thing for any keywords or phrases you use (we talk more about keywords in the SEO chapter).

When you're done, you may have a very colorful document. That's ok! Simply pick one color to start with and go back through your content to adjust the words you use so you can remove the highlighters.

Don't sweat it if there's no way to take out a particular word. Just do your best and adjust what you can.

Voice Recording Tests

When you're done writing a page, read it out loud to yourself and record it. There are free phone apps for this. (I use Voice

Recorder & Audio Editor for the iPhone. You can find it on the Apple store for free.)

After you've recorded yourself reading what you wrote, listen to it. Is it conversational? Is it engaging? Is it boring? You need to consider all these things.

Do not be discouraged. Even if you are not a writer, this does not have to be hard.

Pretend a customer, patient – whoever your target audience is – is standing in front of you. What would you say to them about the topic you are writing about for that page?

Reviews, Testimonials, & Social Proof

Customers, patients, users — whoever you serve — use reviews and testimonials as social proof to show that your people are happy with you and what you offer. This is especially important on your Google Business Profile (more on that later).

If you can add a slider or have reviews embedded on your pages directly (may require help from your agency/third party or a plugin on your CMS), you should do so. It's an effective way to show satisfaction in what you provide.

Proof Your Work

Always, always, always proofread your work. Have someone else proof it. If you've been working on it for a few hours, step away and take a break. Then go back to it with fresh eyes.

It's easy to miss things when you've been staring at your screen for hours.

A website riddled with mistakes will destroy the trust you have built with existing visitors and will make you look unprofessional. It may even give new visitors the perception that your website is not secure.

(By the way, if your website domain doesn't have an SSL security certificate — doesn't have "https:" and a padlock in the browser — then you need to talk to your hosting company.)

7

Formatting & Optimizing is Crucial

I mentioned it before, but better to face it now — people won't read your whole page of content. As I said earlier, you write for both the readers and the skimmers.

Use content that helps you connect to the reader and shows them how savvy you are about their needs and how you can solve their problems.

But you can't do it in block paragraph after block paragraph.

Change it up.

H1, H2, H3 Headers

Break up your content into sections and put them under a header. Remember having to do outlines in high school English or language arts class? That's essentially the idea with your website page.

This falls under the SEO umbrella and keywords, but I want to introduce it here.

Each page of your website needs to include a relevant, unique H1 (Header 1). This is the main title, the main idea of your page. Keep it under 50-60 characters including spaces. It tells the user and search engine what the page is about.

From there, you want to break up your sections using H2s as the next level. Typically, these are a smaller font than the H1 and are the supporting sections for the H1 page topic.

Anything underneath these H2 headers that need to be broken out into other subsections will use an H3, H4, etc. You can have more than one H2, H3 etc. on a page.

Short Paragraphs

I've said it before, and I'll say it again. Keep your paragraphs short.

A good rule is 2-3 sentence rows per paragraph. This isn't like the 4-5 sentences per paragraph blocks that you were told to do in high school or even college. This is writing for digital and cell phones, not printed research papers.

Use a variety of sentence lengths. There's nothing more boring than reading four paragraphs that are styled exactly the same — same length, same lack of energy.

Use short sentences. Use longer sentences when you need to get a larger point across.

And sometimes, you need to use a really long complex sentence to provide the right information for your reader to make sure they understand what you're getting at.

See?

It's even okay to have one line.

Sick of hearing about short and long sentences? Good. It's worth repeating.

Bullets & Numbers

Bulleted lists and numbered lists are great for digital writing. As mentioned earlier, people want fast answers and Google rewards those who offer that. Bullets and numbered lists also get pulled into SERPs, which can include:

- featured snippets
- What People Ask sections
- videos
- knowledge graphs

Learn more about SERPs from Brian Dean's Backlinko.com (link is in the Resources section at the end of the book.)

Photos

Make sure your photos are of good quality and sized to the exact size you need. Sometimes websites will use one centrally located photo and will format it automatically into different shapes for multiple purposes.

For example, a lot of blogs have a large hero image at the top of the blog, and then it gets resized automatically and pulled into a card for related blog sections. In this case, you will need to figure out what your website requires.

Keep in mind that when photos are left or right aligned on desktop, they can sometimes format incorrectly on mobile. You may need to test it out and see what works.

If there is a section after you load the image for vspace or hspace, this means you can put a barrier of space around the image so it doesn't bump right up to the text around it.

Some website systems do this automatically. If not, vspace equals vertical space and hspace is horizontal. You do this in pixels (px). You probably only need like 5px, but you'll determine that when you test it out.

I personally like to have the photo placed in between two paragraphs and have it be sized large enough to look good but not slow the page load too much.

Sometimes a CMS will resize the photo for you and make sure it isn't too large of a file automatically.

Videos

Embedded YouTube videos are a great way to present information. If you have YouTube videos to add to your site, do so strategically and sparingly. Videos can slow down your page load speed.

You can also use a CTA button that says, "Watch Video" and just use the YouTube link in the CTA.

Links

Links are so important. I covered it a little bit in the CTA section, but there are other things to consider.

1. Link Color Contrast

Do not use light colors to show a link on your website, such as a light yellow, gray, or gold. Accessibility is a huge topic when it comes to websites. Contrast is very important.

It's possible, though unlikely, that if someone who can't see the lighter links visits your site and is upset, they could sue you.

I'm not a lawyer. I'm just rationally thinking that the chances of your small business or non-profit having this problem is small.

But why take that chance? It's a bad UX experience regardless of someone's ability to see the contrast.

Make sure whatever link color you use, that it's clear it's a link. Use an underline. (This brings up the point that you shouldn't underline text if it's not a link — even for stylistic purposes.)

You can check your color contrast using the WebAIM: Link Contrast Checker (link in the Resources section). This site also shares other insights that may be helpful.

2. Short Link Text

What does this mean?

Don't link an entire sentence unless it's only a few words. You should link relevant text that tells the reader and search engine what to expect on the other end of that link.

Example: "Do your wallet a solid and check out our women's shirts on clearance before these amazing deals (and shirts) are gone!"

Do not do this: "Do your wallet a solid and check out our women's shirts on clearance before these amazing deals (and shirts) are gone!"

Too many long links like the one above is bad for a few reasons. Have you ever seen a website where there are multiple sentences that are underlined as a link? Was it distracting to you?

It makes your website look outdated. It is also hard to read on mobile. Just don't do it. It's icky and destroys your credibility. (Yes, icky is a super professional term.)

Plus, what you link helps you rank for keywords. You could rank for "women's shirts on clearance". You will not rank for the entire sentence.

Mobile vs Desktop

Desktop views used to be the king of the internet. People would hop on their laptops. Now, we're on the move and cell phones have become king. If you do not format and optimize for mobile first, you need to. Google gives priority to mobile-first websites.

Don't worry though. Your CMS probably already accounts for mobile and desktop. Some are more complicated, but the popular ones like WordPress should already account for that.

This means links, photos, CTAs, paragraphs, column sizes, endless scrolling (not a great UX experience), and navigation need to be functional and look good on mobile.

Different browsers, phone types, laptops, and screen sizes can make your website look and render differently. For the most part this shouldn't be an issue, but you should double check your phone to see how it looks and functions.

You can also use the Chrome extension called Mobile Simulator. It's in the resources section at the end of this book and shows how your website looks on certain phones and laptops.

Note: Some laptop and phone types are free, and others aren't. But the free versions should give you an idea of any issues. You need to be on your website before you click on the extension, and you can choose how you want to view it.

8

Optimize Your Blog

If you have a blog, congratulations! That's a great accomplishment and can really help with your organic SEO. It does need some upkeep though. If you haven't already, apply all the things from this book to your blog.

You will format your blog using these same suggestions in this formatting chapter. You will use the same tactics for the SEO portion you will read in the next chapter.

Here are additional things to consider.

1. Don't make a blog post too short.

I would suggest nothing less than 600 words. According to Backlink.com (one of my favorite SEO websites), blogs closer to 2,000 words rank higher. But Google changes things up and it really is dependent on the industry and topic.

Please do not freak out. You do not need to write this much to have a successful blog! The most important thing is that you're providing your readers with a helpful resource.

As long as the content is relevant and helpful to the reader, it shouldn't matter. But what is the point of a 300-word blog post?

2. Have an interesting and relevant hero image.

Use a strong hero image for your blog. Authentic photos are best, especially if you sell products and can use those photos (make sure they look professional!).

However, there are free photo sites where you don't need to pay a royalty or a monthly fee.

Here are a few:

- Canva (free or paid version)
- Pixabay.com
- Pexels.com
- Unsplash.com
- Shutterstock (paid version)

Make sure you read the rules for each as some may require you to share who took the photo. Some may not. It's always nice to attribute the photographer though. It looks professional, and you never know if it could be a networking opportunity.

If you can't use your own authentic photos, just try to find a photo that includes a person that isn't in cheese mode. There are so many ridiculous stock photos that are clearly staged.

Try to find one that is more natural. If it doesn't make sense to have a person in the photo, do your best to find the right photo to represent the topic of your blog and have it stand out.

3. Resize your photos so they aren't too big.

It's important to have a large enough photo so that it's clear and can be placed nicely in your blog. Don't have the photo be too big of a file or it will slow the load of your page.

Never take a smaller photo and make it bigger. It will be blurry, pixelated, and look terrible.

Use photos throughout your blog if you can and if it makes sense to do so.

If you don't have Photoshop or the skills to use it, I recommend using Canva for resizing or Befunky.com. The free versions do a good job of getting you what you need.

4. Interlink to relevant pages on your website and other blogs.

Interlinking is so crucial and an important on-page SEO element that holds people on your site longer, keeps search engines crawling your site, and helps rank your content higher.

It's possible to go overboard.

You do not need to have 15 links to other pages on one blog post. 2-3 relevant ones are good enough depending on how long your blog is.

Spread the links out and make sure you follow the link tips in the formatting chapter. Most blogs also have a related articles section sorted by topic that automatically pulls into the page, usually at the bottom or in a sidebar.

You can also include in between paragraphs a "Related: [insert title and link title]".

5. Strong external links are also important.

You can get by without having an external link in your blog if there's no reason to. If you're not citing any resources, you may not have an external link to use.

If you're referencing another website, you should link to it though. The only exception would be if it's a bad website. If it's a bad website (unprofessional, not secure, etc.), then ditch it and find a different resource to link.

6. Use strong content. Proofread and quality check all links.

You'll see this part is also something we've talked about already.

Your content needs to be strong and useful, without mistakes. If your blog has misspellings or a lot of mistakes, you can ruin your credibility in the eyes of that reader and search engines.

Check your links to make sure they are accurate and that they work. Put a CTA on the page. If you're talking about a product or service, link back to the product page or the service page.

Include a photo of the product.

7. Your title matters.

Ideally, your title will be 50-60 characters, including spaces. It will have relevant keywords and catch the eye of your reader. Easier said than done, right?

In the next chapter, we'll talk about keywords, which you will use to create your title. You can analyze your title for readability, SEO, and sentiment using free headline and title websites like CapitalizeMyTitle.com.

This site has a lot of popups, but it does give feedback on how to make your titles stronger.

If your blog includes a list of things, like 10 ways to wear a scarf, include 10 in the title and use numbers in the blog. Google loves numbers in titles because they know readers want to easily digest the information quickly and lists are a great way to do that.

10 Fun Ways to Wear Your Scarf this Winter

Include a short paragraph as an introduction to the blog, then start with number 1.

1. Wear it around your head.

Then you would add more content here to explain each number.

You get the idea, right?

Numbers are huge. But don't always use the same number. Don't have 34 blogs that list out 7 things every time.

8. Don't use long URL slugs.

Your website may populate the URL to your blog or page when you add the title. But you can adjust the slug, which is the part of the URL for that specific page. Example: /women-jogger-pants.

Remove stop words like "a", "the", "to" and use the main keywords and ideas if you can. Keep it short. Do this before hitting "Publish".

Note: If you have existing articles published, DO NOT change your URLs. This will break the URL you might be linking to from other pages or that you've posted on social media.

Keep the URLs as they are and focus on making the adjustments to future blogs you post.

9

Harness the Impact of SEO

If you haven't heard about it or seen the acronym SEO thrown around (Search Engine Optimization), it is a very broad topic with a lot of moving parts, updates, and different categories.

Technical SEO

Technical SEO deals with sitemaps, robots.txt files, site indexing, schema, broken links, 404 pages, URL redirects, and other non-creative types of things that are important for your website. They are handled more in the backend and many website systems take care of this for you.

Programs for technical SEO include:

- Google Search Console
- GA4 (formerly Google Analytics)
- Ahrefs
- SEMrush
- Screaming Frog

- Google Tag Manager

Someone well-versed in technical SEO usually runs a lot of reports, looks at a lot of data, checks for errors, things like that. It takes a different kind of skill set.

On-page SEO

On-page SEO is my favorite because it deals with content, formatting, and the UX experience. That's what this whole book is about. On-page SEO includes keywords, meta descriptions and title tags, alt tags, headers, and basically anything a visitor to your site can see.

Keyword Research

There are software tools you can use to search for keywords to help boost the organic search findability with your content, your headers, and your formatting. Although many of them require a subscription, there are other ways you can look for keywords and what people search without having to pay anything. Those are my favorite, especially if you have a low to no budget.

Years and years and years ago, you would have to use the keyword phrase verbatim — exactly as people typed it in their search. This would include versions of the words being mis-spelled, not capitalized properly, using hyphens or no hyphens. You get the picture.

It was a mess. And confusing.

Now, Google (not to exclude other search engines) is so much smarter. You don't even need the exact words because Google understands the intent.

If you've ever seen the movie *iRobot* with Will Smith, Sonny is the robot who is different from all the other robots. He can dream. He understands emotions. He understands intent.

Right or wrong, that's how I envision Google — as Sonny the Robot.

The reason I personify Google is because it helps me understand how Google operates. Yes, there's this whole technical thing going on in the background that includes algorithms and data and code.

My brain doesn't comprehend all that. I'm more of the creative type. Maybe you're the same way.

Sonny (Google) knows the topic or keyword phrase I enter in my search bar encompasses a much broader spectrum. For example, if I'm searching for office chairs, Google will find websites that sell office chairs.

But it isn't looking for 'office chairs' specifically in that word order. It could pull up websites that sell 'desk chairs'. It uses the words around the keywords to understand what's on that page.

So, although keywords are really important and can be telling for what your audience is looking for, it's not the be all end all.

What's more important is that you have quality, helpful content on your pages and it's clear what the page is about.

Generally, if you write about a topic, a service, or a product you offer, you will naturally hit those keywords. Yes, there is the whole competition of ranking. SEO professionals will argue that until their last breath.

Shorter keywords are harder to rank for because they are more popular. Longer keyword phrases — called long-tail keywords — have less competition and still get the point across.

For example, the search for 'office chairs' is probably more competitive than 'office chairs with heated seats'. It's a more focused search. Of course, don't hold me to that. Every keyword, every phrase, every location is different. But you get my point.

If one website has more pages, quality content, and is optimized, they may have a higher domain authority, which means they are a more trusted site. Chances are they will rank higher than you if you don't.

But that's okay. SEO is a long game. You may get a few quick wins, but over time, SEO can really impact your website traffic. It's always working for you – for free. And we all love that.

Here are some things you can do to find keywords.

SEOquake Google Extension

Get out your digital binoculars and check out your competitors again. SEOquake is a free Chrome extension (there are some paid features) that can tell you what's going on with a web page.

Once you have SEOquake pinned on your browser, visit a competitor's website, and hit the SQ extension. If you go to "Page Info", it will show you keywords on that page, including ones that are more than one word.

The "Diagnosis" tab shows you the meta and title tag they use, their headers, and other information that is helpful.

You won't understand everything in this extension — there's technical jargon and it's not 100% accurate. But it is a starting point for you and a good way to see how your competitors are optimizing — or not optimizing — their sites.

Google Browser & Local City or Zip Code

You can also use your Google search browser and type in a product or service you offer, include your city, or zip code and see what shows up. Look at other websites' title tags and meta descriptions from the list to get an idea of keywords you can use for your own website.

I saw websites that used the keyword 'office furniture', which proves that Google (or Sonny) understands an office chair falls under the office furniture category.

Another example: I typed 'office chairs Chicago'. What came up were a bunch of sponsored websites for national brands, which makes sense because Chicago is a big city. But I also saw local places in Chicago selling office chairs.

You know what else I found in a "Searches related to office chairs in Chicago"?

- Executive chairs
- Ergonomic office chairs
- Cheap office chairs
- Home office chairs
- Reclining office chairs
- New and used office furniture
- 10 Best Office Chairs for 2023

Google Search & Auto-Populating

A lot of times when you type something in the search bar, Google will auto populate additional searches for that topic. Amazon does this same thing, and you could try Amazon just to get more keywords you wouldn't otherwise think about.

When I type in 'office chair' into the Google search bar, a list below it populates with:

- Office chairs on sale office depot.com
- Office chairs desk chairs
- Office chairs amazon

In this instance above, I would use 'desk chairs' as an additional keyword phrase I can use on my website. Having additional keyword phrases gives your website variety and helps alleviate keyword stuffing.

Keyword stuffing is an old SEO tactic back when the keywords needed to be verbatim what people searched for, like I talked about earlier. If you keyword stuff, Google will ding you for it and could dock you in search results. It can also be a distraction for your users.

These are just three easy ways you can find additional keywords by just using your Google browser. Without spending a dime.

Yes, it can take some time to do this research. I would suggest setting a timer for an hour with the understanding that after that hour, you will take what you've found and run with it.

It's so easy to get sucked into the research portion and then find yourself with too much information that it's overwhelming.

People Ask Section

Your goal is to have quality content that provides answers to people's questions. Another feature where you can pull content ideas and keywords from is the 'People Ask' section. If you search for a term, topic, or phrase, many times there is an accordion that pops up, typically above the organic search results for websites, sometimes in between.

These are questions people ask that Google will pull snippets from someone's website that answers their question. If you open one accordion and close it, more will pop up below it.

You used to be able to create an FAQ page and list those questions on the page and answer them. That's frowned upon now in the SEO community. But what you can do is write down the questions that relate to what you do or what you offer and find a way to work in the information surrounding their question.

Because we're not using a software tool, we don't know the search volume or competitive level. But that's okay. It's easy for people to get caught up in those numbers.

Sometimes people can't move forward because they are stuck on the fact that their particular keyword or product or service is very competitive.

I'm not saying the search volume or competitive levels aren't important. What I am saying is sometimes the keyword 'office chair' is the simplest, most direct way to explain a product.

But you would be sprinkling in other longer keyword phrases anyway, so you're not relying just on 'office chair' to rank.

Answer the Public

You can also use the website Answer the Public. With a free trial, you get three daily searches and can input your topic, product, or service and see what people are asking. (See link in Resources section.)

Google Keyword Planner for Local Keywords

Another useful (and free) Google tool is the Keyword Planner. You can sign up using your Gmail. It will ask you for your billing country and the currency type, but if you're not running ads, you don't need to put in any credit card information.

This is a great way to find keywords searched in your local area because you will input your city and even surrounding cities if you want to expand your reach.

Now what do you do with these keywords? You sprinkle them throughout where it makes sense. Don't make it awkward. Don't force it. Make it natural. Use them in your headers.

Google Trends

You could use Google Trends to determine if one version of a word or phrase is used more than another in a particular area. Use the "Explore" tab. Make sure you use the "search topic". For example, you can see if people in your city or across the country (or internationally too) search for "mobile phone" or "cell phone" more often.

The only thing Google Trends doesn't show you is the search volume. They show the numbers in terms of percentages. So, out of 100% of the time, for the time frame you set, people search for "cell phone" 75% of the time more than "mobile phone".

In addition, if there is enough data available, it can breakdown the search queries even more for you and show you what areas of the location search one over the other.

See more free keyword research tools in the resource section at the end of this book.

Utilize Your Headers & Break Up Content

As mentioned in the formatting chapter, you need headers on your page. A unique H1 for every page, as well as H2s, H3s and so on where appropriate. What you will do is use your keyword list and utilize them where you can in your headers.

Example: 5 Most Popular Ergonomic Office Chairs

List the top 5 ergonomic chairs you sell with an explanation of why people love them and list them out 1-5.

Also in the formatting chapter, write your content using bullets where you can, numbers where it makes sense, short paragraphs, short and long sentences, photos, customer testimonials, etc.

Title Tags & Meta Descriptions

Let's talk about metadata. It sounds technical and scary but it's not.

Title

Anytime you do a Google search, you see the list of websites with linked titles and short descriptions underneath. The titles have SEO value so you want to make sure you're using relevant keywords, sometimes your city and state, and your brand or company name.

Here's an example if you have a local store and don't sell products online (you should consider doing so though!): Women's

Jogging Pants | Rochester, MN | Best Pants Ever, LLC **(60 characters)**

If you ship nationally: Women's Jogging Pants | Free Shipping | Best Pants Ever, LLC **(60 characters)**

If your webpage is about jeans, you better have jeans in your title tag.

Keep your title to 50-60 characters including spaces.

Meta Description

Your meta description should be clear, concise, and include your city if you're local, online shopping if you offer it, and any other pertinent information that can catch a potential visitor's eye.

Keep the meta between 150-170 characters with spaces.

Example: See for yourself why our women's jogging pants from Best Pants Ever are a customer favorite. These soft joggers come in 15 colors and range in size from XS-XXL. **(161 characters)**

Depending on what CMS you're using and if you have an SEO plugin like Yoast, there will be guides to show you when you're over the character limit. Some allow you to have larger character counts. Do what you can to stay between the limits shown above.

The meta description has no SEO ranking value. It is all for the user. It tells them what the page is about. You'll see a lot of companies don't utilize metas for their pages.

If you don't write one, what will happen?

Google may write it for you, typically pulling information from your first paragraph. Or pulling something irrelevant from the page.

Other times, even when you do write them and add them to your website, Google may change them because they think that they know better. (Remember when I said Google has too much power?)

Think about it. If you're looking for something on Google, are you more likely to click on a website that has a clear description of what you can expect to see or one that has nonsense?

It's okay. I know your answer.

Use this opportunity to tell your potential visitors what you offer for that page. This is really important.

Note: Your title and meta may render differently in different browsers, on desktop or on mobile. Don't worry about it. Keep it between the character count provided above, and you should be fine. If your title gets cut off in one browser versus another, on mobile versus desktop, it's okay.

Another thing to keep in mind with your meta and title tag is every page must be unique from another page on your site. If you have pages with the same information, Google won't know which page to rank. So, it won't rank either one.

That goes for any page with duplicate content.

Good luck with writing your metas and titles! You can do this.

Alt Tags & Image File Names

If you have photos or visuals on your site, you need to include an alt tag. When you load the image on your site, it should give you an option to add one. Alt tags are important for accessibility, the user experience, and SEO.

If it's simply a graphic for artistic purposes, like a flower design on the side or another decorative element, you don't need to add anything. I always add an alt tag for logos, so if my company name is Best Pants Ever, I'll put that in the alt tag.

Alt tags are read by software programs for those who visit your site and are blind or don't see well. It allows them to understand what's on your website. So, any products or photos should include an alt tag.

It's also a great way to include keywords for search engines to crawl.

Keep your alt tags brief. In many cases: "Women's black jogger pants" or "Woman smiling at friend over a coffee cup" is sufficient.

Also, name your image files using keywords as well. If you get an image from a royalty free site, change the title of the file to something that is keyword-rich like: Coffee-Shop-Chicago.

10

Questions to Ask Your SEO Pro or Agency

Do you have someone managing your website? Maybe an SEO pro or a writer?

Maybe you have an agency running things for you. If you do, that's great. Hopefully the expense is worth it and allows you to focus on your company, nonprofit, or whatever it is you do.

These questions can be more of an informational resource for you or a check-up to make sure your agency or SEO person is doing what they should.

Note: Check your contract with them to see if they will charge you to answer your questions.

Here are things you can ask:

1. Is there a sitemap?

- A sitemap includes all webpages on your site and tells Google and other search engines what your site is about, what pages are included, etc. It's important. Even if you have a small website.
- The CMS you use may create the sitemap automatically, but there are instances when an agency or SEO person will do this.
- You can see if there is a sitemap by putting this at the end of your homepage URL in the browser: /sitemap.xml or /sitemap_index.xml
- For example: https://fakewebsite.com/sitemap.xml

2. Is there a robots.txt?

- A robots.txt file speaks to search engines and tells them if there are pages that shouldn't be crawled or indexed. This could be a blog, product search results page, or a patient portal.
- You can check if a robots.txt file is on your site by putting /robots.txt after the URL.
- Example: https://fakewebsite.com/robots.txt
- Possible follow up question: What is being blocked by robots?

5. Is there schema added to the pages?

This is another technical SEO tactic that speaks to search engines and a way to potentially have Google put your page in a snippet in organic search.

Schema also has a local SEO impact. (Yes, another type of SEO.)

It's most important on your main pages and is a code put in the header of the page on the back end, so you won't see it just by looking at your site.

- You can test for yourself if there is schema added to a particular page.
- Visit: https://validator.schema.org/ and input the URL of the page. If results show up on the right-hand side of the page, then it probably has some sort of schema.
- Your CMS may automatically create schema when you publish a page.

4. Is there analytics set up on your site?

This will typically be GA4. Hopefully you are getting regular analytics reports from them. Ask for access as well if you don't already have it.

GA4 will tell you how many site views you have, how many new and returning users, what device they use to view your site, their engagement time, etc. If you have a blog, you can see how it performs. You can see what your main pages are that people visit.

There are tons of great insights you can get that can inform you of additional ways to optimize your site, add more content, etc.

GA4 is something you need to learn how to use. Usually, if you have a small site, you only need to know how to check pages and a basic overview of data. There are plenty of online resources for this.

5. If GA4 is implemented, ask what events are set up for tracking.

An event is an action a user takes on your site. If a person clicks on the CTA of a product, or an email sign up CTA for instance, then that is tracked. It gives you an idea of what people are doing on your site.

6. Are there any broken links and 404 pages?

If you have a larger website, like maybe you have an e-commerce site that has a lot of pages and links, you can ask your agency or SEO person to run a Screaming Frog scan if they have that software, or an Ahrefs scan or SEMrush scan – it depends on which software they have.

Tip: If possible, create your 404 page (broken link page) creative — add a graphic, use clever language (if you can make someone chuckle, they typically will forgive you for having a broken link). Add a link back to that section page or homepage, whatever makes sense.

Note: They may charge you for this time and service.

These software platforms can help find broken links you didn't know you had and other technical issues. It can also tell you if you have missing metas or titles.

6. Is Google Search Console set up for your site?

GSC is a tool that allows you to see the search queries people use that get them to your site. It also shows which pages are indexed, which aren't, and other technical things.

If a page isn't indexed and should be, this is where you can request indexing of the page. It's also where you can ask for reindexing if you make major changes to a page.

When you make the changes to your site, you can request reindexing. If you don't, Google will continue to crawl your site, and it will eventually be reindexed. It's a continuous thing.

Your sitemap should also be included on GSC.

7. If you have someone do keyword research, ask to see what terms they are targeting.

They should be able to provide a list of keyword terms and phrases they used on your site from Google.

8. Ask to see a list of the metas and title tags they wrote for your pages if you didn't do them yourself.

You can also check yourself by visiting a page and using the SEOquake extension.

11

Local SEO & Google Business Profile

Here's a little extra bonus for you that deals with local findability. (Local SEO.)

Google Business Profile (GBP) — formerly known as Google My Business — helps with local SEO and being found in your area if you are a service-based company or have a brick-and-mortar location. Most types of industries can utilize this free service from Google. (Another free option!)

You may already have one of these, and if you do, fantastic! Hopefully you have all the right information in there and it's working for you. If not, I'm going to tell you about it briefly.

There is so much content on the internet about GBP, and I'll add it to the Resources section at the bottom to help you further.

This is a listing for your company or service that pops up on the right-hand side with the right search query in your local area. It includes your address, website, hours, services, industry type, photos, directions, maps, reviews, posts, events, a description, and other things depending on the industry you're in. Some features aren't available for some services.

The goal is to get your business listing at the top of the map pack. In an organic search, the map pack is the list of businesses and their directions, etc. that typically comes before any unsponsored websites.

If you can get into the top spot in your local area for the product or service you provide, chances are you will get the most traffic.

If you're lower down on the list, you have things you can do to work your way up the pack. Reviews are an important part of that. That's another topic entirely.

Some quick tips:

- Make sure your company name matches the name of your GBP business listing
- Fill in everything you can in the GBP
- Add photos
- Add a description
- Add hours, phone, website, etc.
- Get as many reviews as you can naturally
- Depending on the industry, you can add products or services
- You can add posts and events

GBP gets suspicious if it thinks you are doing shady things to get reviews and could suspend your listing.

Also, on your Contact Us page or Locations page on your website, you want to embed the GBP map on your website and link back to it with the directions link. If you have two locations, you should have two GBP listings.

Note: They make you verify the listing and sometimes it's a bit cumbersome. Usually, it's a video. They used to send postcards but not as much anymore. They may just give you a call, too.

You also want to be on Bing Places (not as good as GBP) and Apple Maps. Both are kind of a process, but many people use their default map app from their phone. You want to make sure they can find you regardless of which app they use.

12

Last Thoughts

By now you should have a bunch of ideas on how you can improve and optimize your website for both your users and search engines. The goal is to help your audience find you. A higher Google ranking can bring in more website traffic.

Of course, I'm not guaranteeing results. I can't do that. Your success is dependent on a lot of factors that I have nothing to do with. My hope is that you will take these (free) tools I've provided and actionable items you can do yourself to improve your website.

Don't get overwhelmed! You can do this. And remember, keep it simple. Do a little at a time if needed.

Conduct other research to learn more about these topics. There's so much information available that doesn't cost a thing.

Thank you for reading this book. If you're satisfied with the tips and resources I provided you, I'd be eternally grateful if

you left a review!

Good luck to you and happy optimizing!

13

Resources

SEO Resources

My favorite resources for SEO

- Brian Dean from Backlinko.com: https://backlinko.com/
- Learn more about SERPs: https://backlinko.com/hub/seo/serps
- Neil Patel from Ubersuggest: https://neilpatel.com/ubersuggest/
- Subscribe to these guys. It's worth it.

SEO Title Checker: https://capitalizemytitle.com/headline-analyzer/

BrightLocal: Local SEO & Competitor Research: https://www.brightlocal.com/free-local-seo-tools/

Yoast or equivalent plugin on your CMS

Meta & Title Tag Previewer: https://chromewebstore.google.c
om/detail/mobile-simulator-responsi/ckejmhbmlajgoklhgba
pkiccekfoccmk

Keywords Research

- Ubersuggest (free but limited): https://neilpatel.com/uber
  suggest/
- Answer the Public: https://answerthepublic.com/ (Also
  from Neil Patel — helps with customer research, SEO topics,
  etc. Free 3 searches per day)
- Moz: https://moz.com/free-seo-tools (Limited free tools)
- Ahrefs: https://ahrefs.com/free-seo-tools (Limited free
  tools)
- SEMrush: https://www.semrush.com/ (Limited free tools
  — go through the steps but select "skip trial")
- Google Trends: https://trends.google.com/trends/
- Google Ads Keyword Planner Local Research: https://ads.g
  oogle.com/home/

Technical SEO Resources (may overlap with other SEO tools)

- Google Search Console: https://search.google.com/search-
  console/about
- GA4 (formerly Google Analytics): https://analytics.withgo
  ogle.com/
- Ahrefs: https://ahrefs.com/free-seo-tools
- SEMrush: https://www.semrush.com/
- Screaming Frog: https://www.screamingfrog.co.uk/seo-s
  pider/ (Limited free tools)
- Google Tag Manager: https://tagmanager.google.com/

- Schema Checker: https://validator.schema.org/

UX & Accessibility Resources

- Link contrast checker & other Accessibility rules: https://webaim.org/resources/linkcontrastchecker/

Content & Photos

Royalty free photos

- Canva (free or paid version): https://www.canva.com/
- Pixabay: https://pixabay.com/
- Pexels: https://www.pexels.com/
- Unsplash: https://unsplash.com/
- Shutterstock: https://www.shutterstock.com/

Spelling, Grammar, & Plagiarism Check

- Use your Word Doc or Google Doc tools!
- Grammarly free version: https://www.grammarly.com/grammar-check
- Plagiarism Check: https://www.grammarly.com/plagiarism-checker

ChatGPT: https://chat.openai.com/

Passive vs Active Voice https://www.grammarly.com/blog/active-vs-passive-voice/

Writing for the web https://www.semrush.com/blog/14-tips-for-writing-awesome-website-content/

Business Listings & Map Apps

Google Business Profile: https://www.google.com/business/

- YouTube: https://www.youtube.com/watch?v=RBi9CPWE HEo
- GBP Support: https://support.google.com/business/answe r/2911778?hl=en&co=GENIE.Platform%3DDesktop

Bing Places: https://www.bingplaces.com/

Apple Maps: https://businessconnect.apple.com/

www.ingramcontent.com/pod-product-compliance
Lightning Source LLC
LaVergne TN
LVHW051612050326
832903LV00033B/4466